C

A Paradigm Parable

AND THE BOX

Frank A. Prince

Jossey-Bass
Pfeiffer
San Francisco

Copyright © 1993 by Jossey-Bass/Pfeiffer

Editors: JoAnn Padgett and Katharine Pechtimaldjian; Interior Graphic Designer: Paul Bond; Cover: John Odam Design Associates

Prince, Frank A.
    C and the Box: a paradigm parable / by Frank A. Prince.
      p. cm.
    ISBN 0-89384-226-5 (pbk.)
    1. Creative thinking. 2. Creative ability. 3. Creative ability in business. I. Title
  BF408.P73   1993
  153.3'5—dc20   92-51021

ISBN: Paper 0-89384-226-5   Hardcover 0-88390-364-4

Printed in the United States of America

Published by

Jossey-Bass
Pfeiffer

350 Sansome Street, 5th Floor
San Francisco, California 94104-1342
(415) 433-1740; Fax (415) 433-0499
(800) 274-4434; Fax (800) 569-0443

Visit our website at: http://www.pfeiffer.com

Outside of the United States, Pfeiffer products can be purchased from the following Simon & Schuster International Offices:

Prentice Hall
Campus 400
Maylands Avenue
Hemel Hempstead
Hertfordshire HP2 7EZ
United Kingdom
44(0) 1442 881891; Fax 44(0) 1442 882074

Prentice Hall Professional
Locked Bag 507
Frenchs Forest PO NSW 2086
Australia
61 2 9454 2200; Fax 61 2 9453 0089

Simon & Schuster (Asia) Pte Ltd
317 Alexandra Road
#04–01 IKEA Building
Singapore 159965
Asia
65 476 4688; Fax 65 378 0370

Prentice Hall/Pfeiffer
P.O. Box 1636
Randburg 2125
South Africa
27 11 781 0780; Fax 27 11 781 0781

Printing 10 9 8 7 6

C went to school and learned the shape of a box.

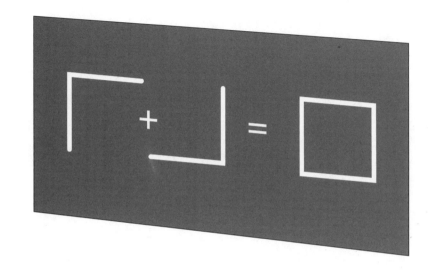

After years in school, C honed and refined the shape of the box and was quite certain about it.

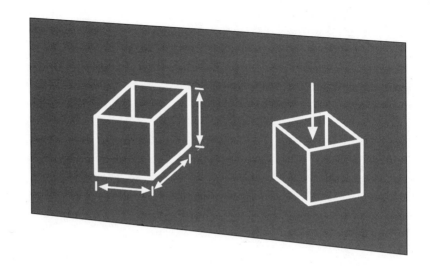

C graduated from school and started a career.

C discovered that the new job had an invisible box. Through trial and error though, C found all of the sides and knew what was in and what was out.

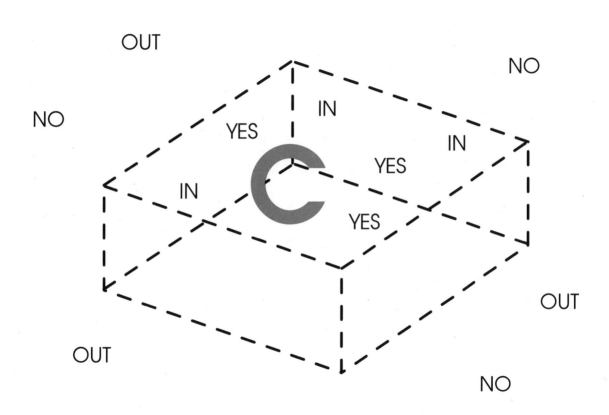

C was proud.

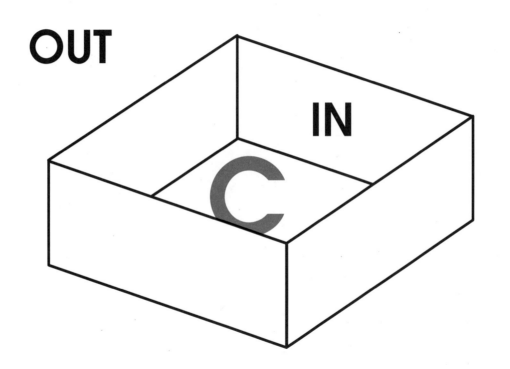

All of C's time at work was spent in the box.

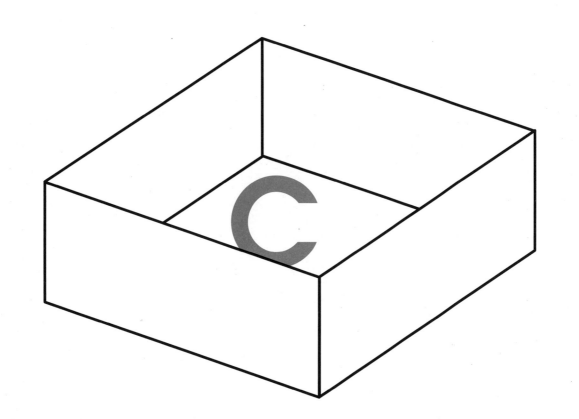

It was comfortable inside the box.

C was good at the work to be done inside the box as long as it didn't change.

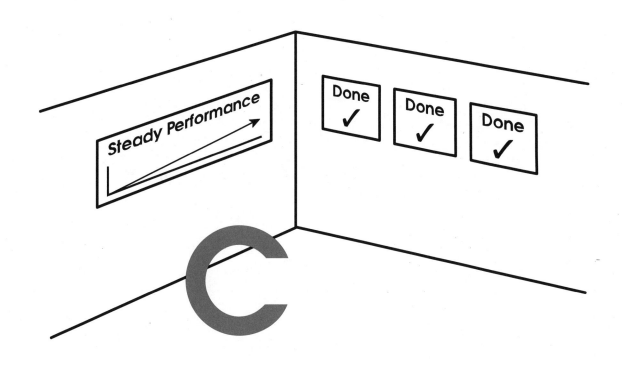

C could do everything inside the box without much thought.

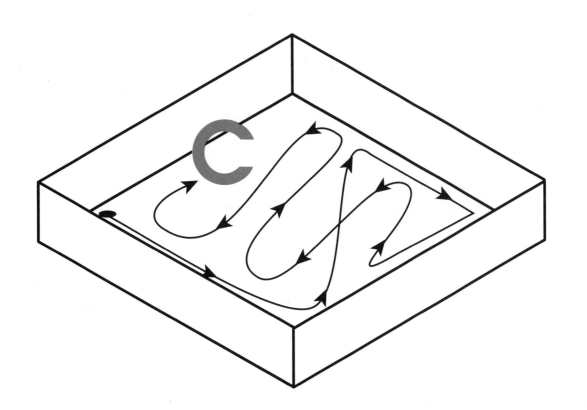

C could even do it with closed eyes.

C could do it without thinking.

C got bored...

C knew every inch of the box. But one day C found a dusty old spring.

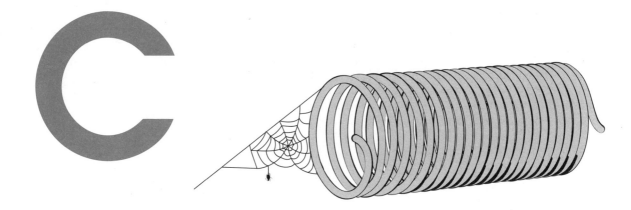

It had a tag on it that said it was part of C's box.

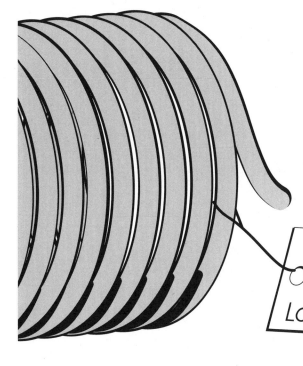

Part #3047893475913

OWNER: C

Location: Box 4-A #3187

C had not needed the spring before and could do everything without it.

C tried to throw it out, but the sides of the box were too high.

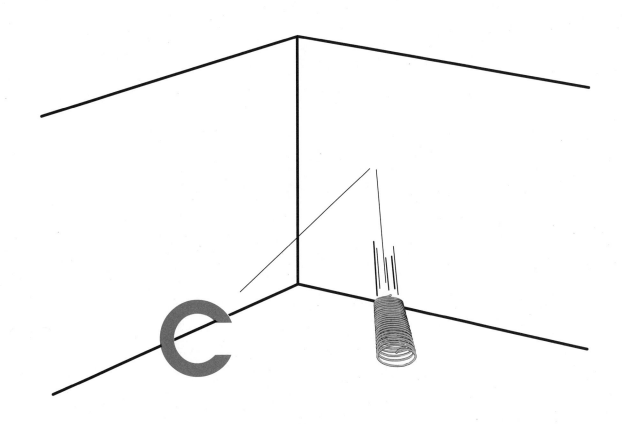

C wondered how the walls had become so high and realized that extended use of the box caused deep ruts to form along the borders.

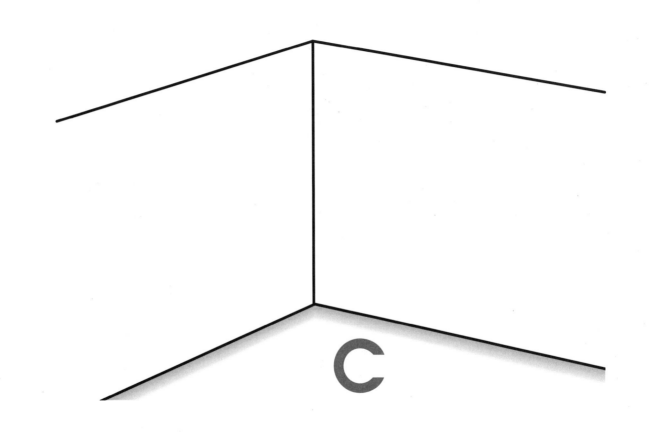

The ruts were so deep that C couldn't see outside of the box.

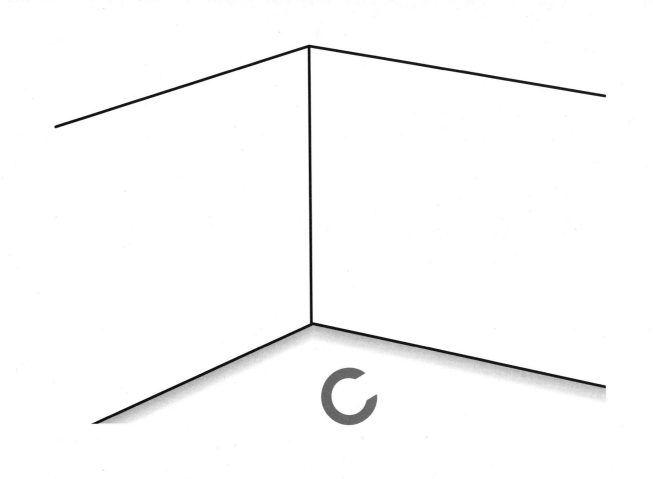

C had even forgotten that there was an outside to the box.

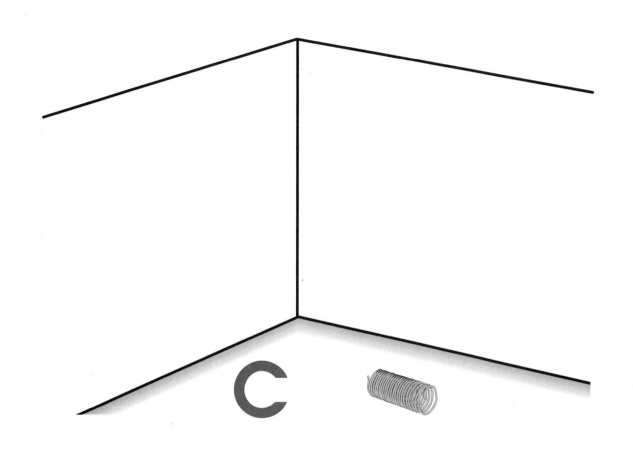

C threw the spring into the corner but kept running into it.

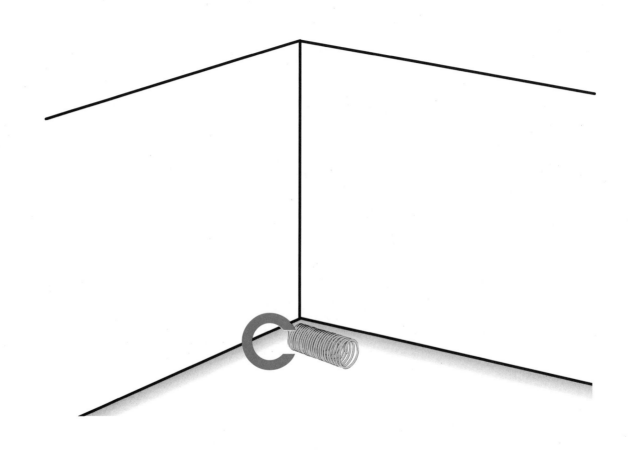

C became intrigued by the spring.

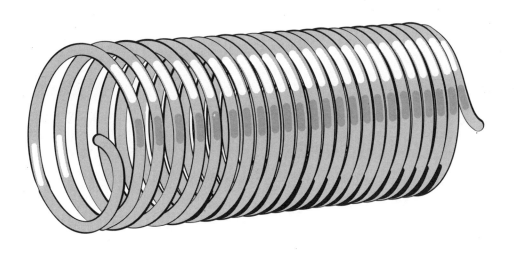

C's mind kept wandering back to the spring, since C's job could be done without thinking hard.

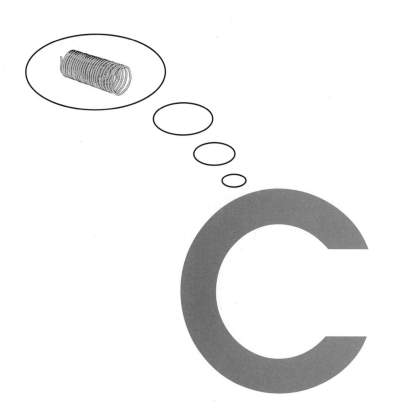

C thought, "How might I use the spring?"...But the spring just sat there and did nothing.

One day out of frustration and boredom, C threw the spring.

Then C kicked it.

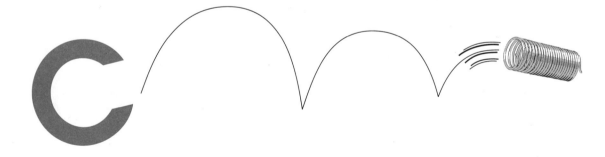

Finally, C jumped on the spring.

And it sprang C right out of the box!

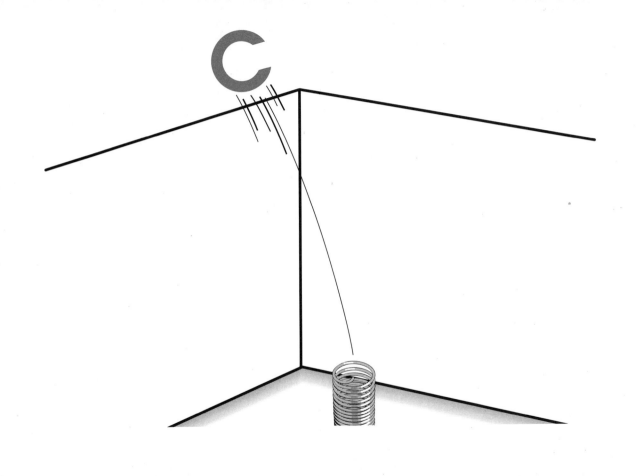

C got scared and quickly jumped back into the box.

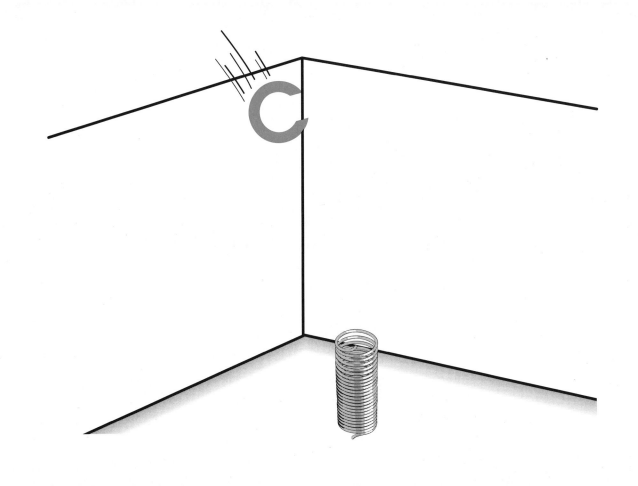

But C landed on the spring, and it bounced C out the other side.

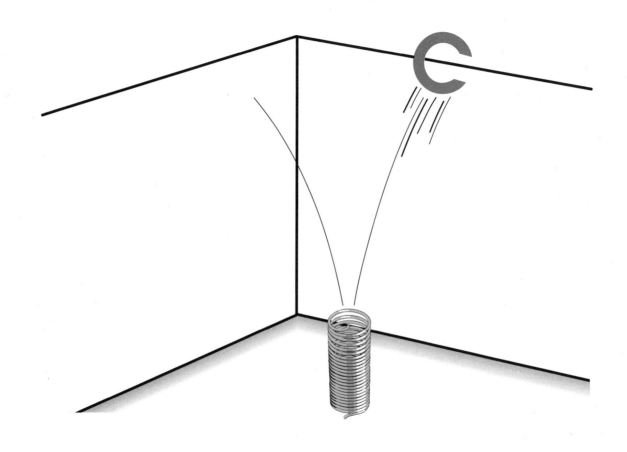

Except this time it was fun.

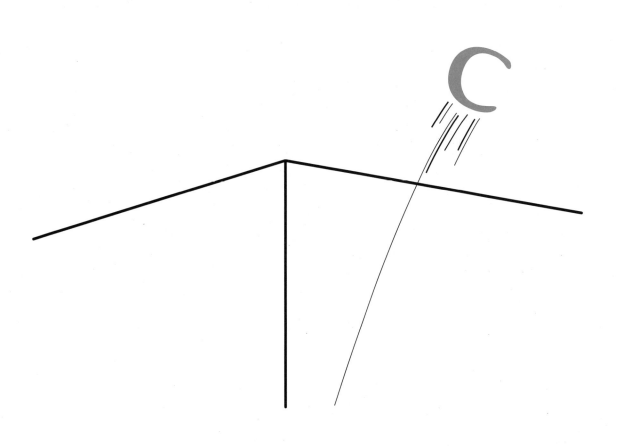

So C tried it again.

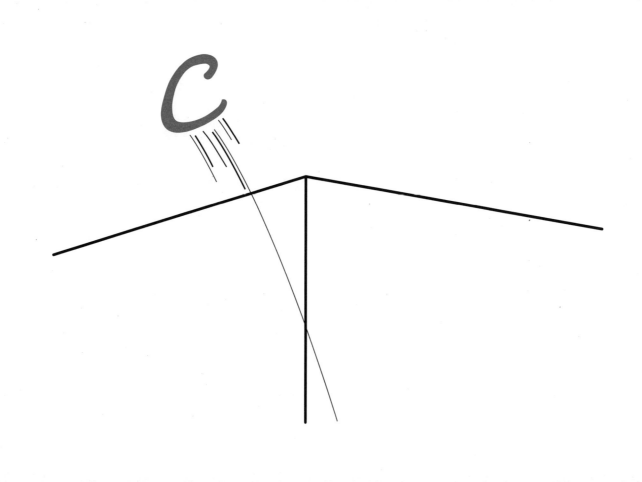

...and again.

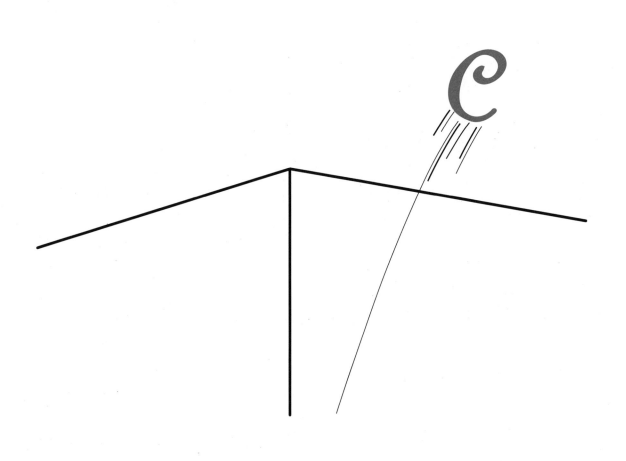

It was lots of fun!

As the days passed by, C was able to work in and out of the box whenever C wanted.

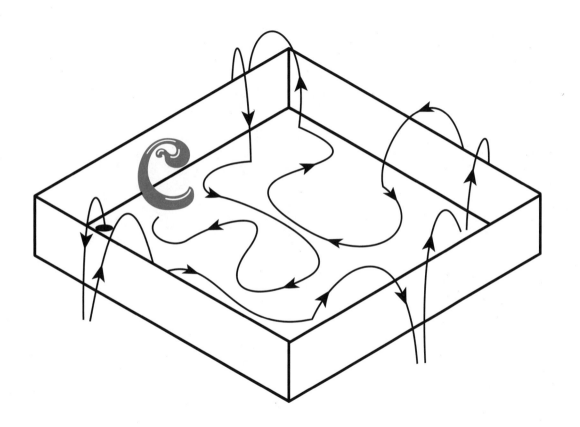

C even got comfortable being outside of the box.

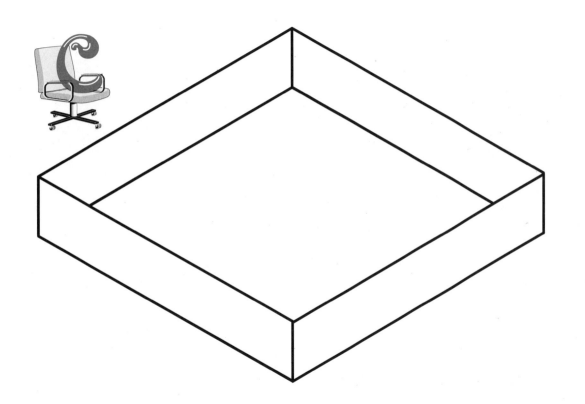

C felt like a child again.

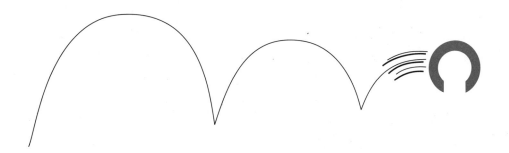

C looked forward each day to going to work
and doing things in and out of the box.

The other workers did not know about C's spring. Everyone just thought C was different than them.

They thought C was born that way. It was easy for C to be creative; they were not creative.

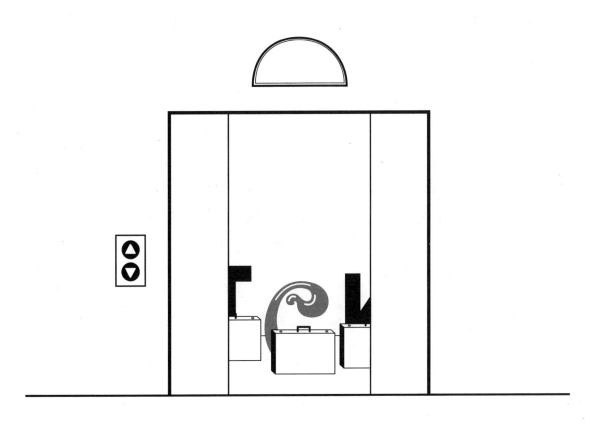

They knew C was always coming up with new and different ways to do work and to have fun. C's box seemed to be getting bigger and bigger.

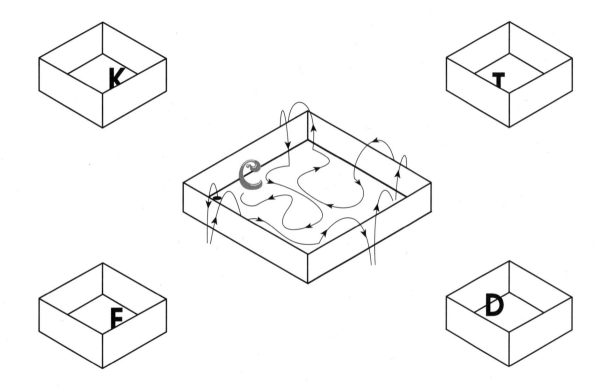

C told co-workers about the special spring and suggested that their boxes might have one too.

KDTF

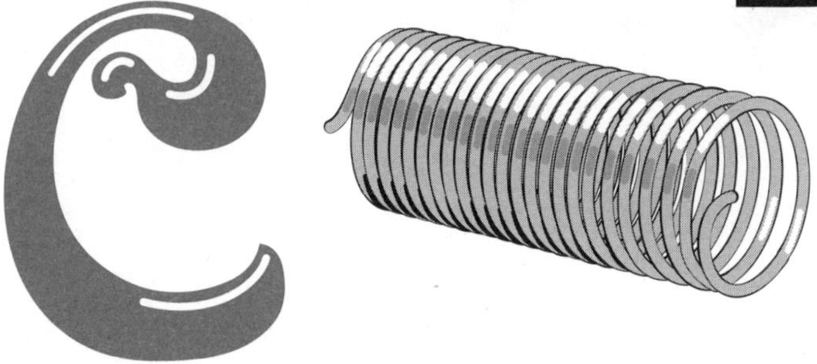

They searched and found that they all had a special spring in their boxes.

 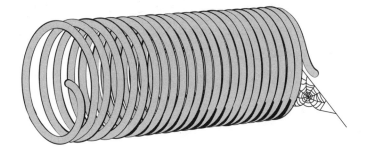

Many of them remembered using a spring when they were children, but they had forgotten how fun it was and how to use it.

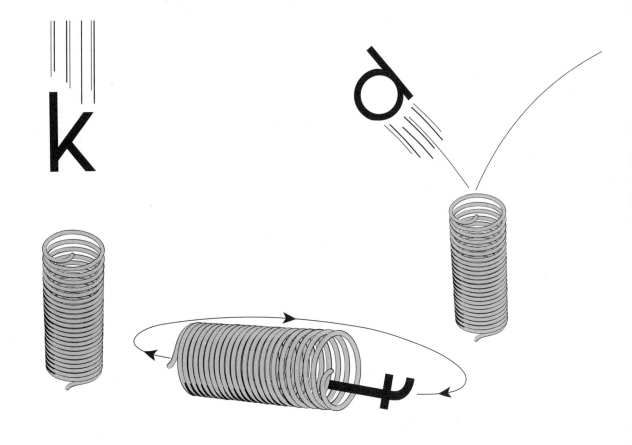

Before long, they were all working in and out of their boxes.

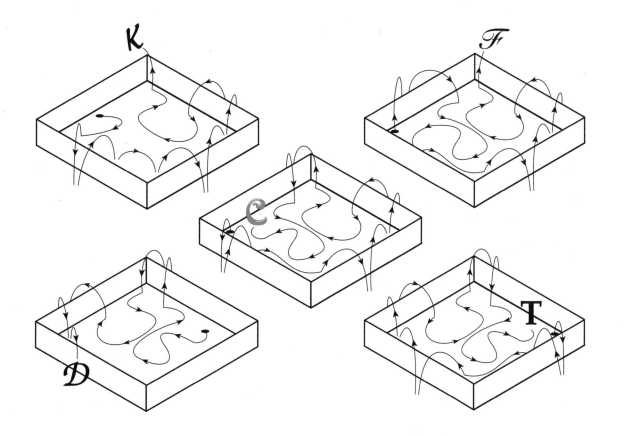

Boxes were growing and eventually everyone was enjoying their work. They even started working together.

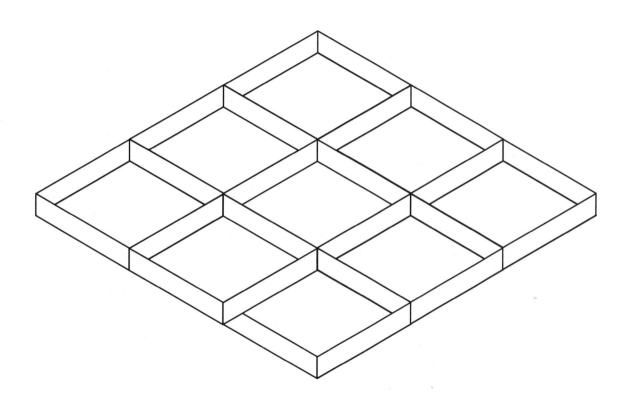

C became the hero of the company.

C reflected back on how such an environment was created.

It was simple. All C had done was to give them something they already had.

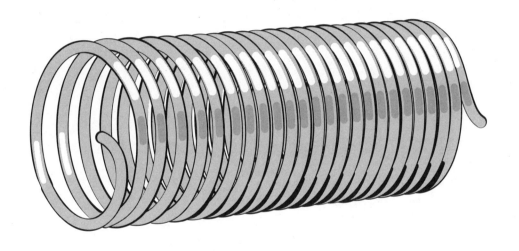

We are all born with this spring, but we use it less and less as we search to define the box.

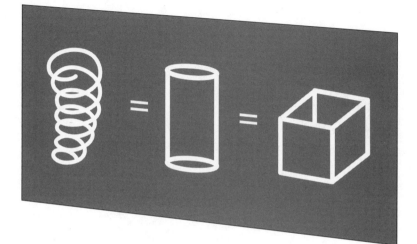

C

One day, while contentedly polishing the spring, C wondered...

How might we keep from losing such a valuable tool as our spring as we grow up?

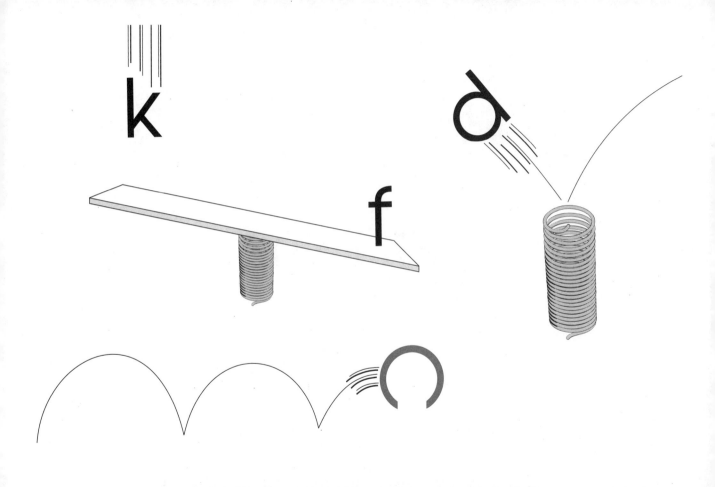

THE END

Epilogue

As young children, we were highly creative and adventurous. We knew no boundaries and would play, experiment, question, and use our imagination in the most wondrous of ways. Over time, we learned the "right way to do things." We learned to look for the *one* right answer to problems. We were even tested on knowing the right answer. It was not okay to be different.

We never really lose our imagination and creativity. We just don't take it out and use it, practice it, play with it, or develop it. As a result, many of us now operate within an area that is known and comfortable. Outside of that comfortable "box" is a wonderful area to be explored. You just have to find ways to step outside. When was the last time you practiced using your imagination? Try doing it once a day. Then twice a day or more! When you are faced with a problem, try exploring solutions that would be impossible to do. Force yourself to find at least ten alternative ways to do something before you do it. Remember, exploration outside of the box may not be comfortable. It may not seem possible or even practical. But, if you practice going there enough times, you will experience the motivation that drives the true explorers! The following pages offer some ideas to get you started.

How can you be more creative?

- Take a five-minute imagination break each morning and afternoon.
- Spend an entire day without judging anything or anyone.
- Share what you like about an idea first.
- Try to invent a new product once a week.
- Pretend you are chairperson of the board for one day.
- Use candy as imaginary brain-power pills in a meeting.
- Present information graphically versus in writing.

- Make a list of possible options before making a choice.
- Take fun breaks.
- Share your hobbies at work.
- Encourage experimentation.
- Trade jobs with a co-worker for a day.
- Think of a terrible solution to a problem, then find something positive about the solution.
- Draw pictures or doodle.
- Find a new word and use it in speech or correspondence.
- Suggest ideas that seem like long shots.
- Look for at least five positive answers to problems.
- Try to learn a musical instrument.
- Create a piece of art.
- If you always read fiction, read nonfiction for a change.
- Listen to the radio instead of watching television.

- Jump in a puddle.
- Run barefoot in wet grass.
- Read a favorite children's story again.
- Look through a kaleidoscope.
- Fingerpaint all of your holiday cards.
- Climb a tree.
- Make a new recipe with a food you have never prepared before.
- Lay in a field and watch the clouds.

If you have other ideas you'd like to share, we'd welcome your creativity. Please send your thoughts to Pfeiffer.

About the Author

Frank Prince is cofounder of the consulting firm, Involvement Systems, Inc. As an international motivational speaker, management consultant, and author, Frank has the ability to spark a creative spirit within individuals and groups. He has done pioneering work in team development and in moving groups toward high performance. Frank started up several new manufacturing facilities under team-based, participative management structures. Frank is used by many organizations to facilitate "out of the box" thinking in such areas as strategic planning, reengineering, or new product development. He also works at the individual level and has trained over 5,000 people at all levels of organizations in the use of creativity.

Frank is also an accomplished artist working in oils and acrylics. To balance his creative side, Frank has a degree in Engineering. On the wilder side, Frank enjoys racing off-road motorcycles, free climbing, and mountain biking as modes of experiential learning.

Mr. Prince is available for speaking engagements and workshops. He can be reached at Involvement Systems, Inc., 10635 Buccaneer Point, Frisco, Texas 75034, (214) 625-1099.